" Hail Queen Mother Mary, Our
dearest Lord, Mother Earth,,
Blessed With A son to whom
shall be celebrated by birth on
Christmas day. The day
prophetic beings are born..

Los Dos Velas,,

Born December 25th.
Honor The First hero and
proud father of your Prophet
of today's salvation. The First
father of the Demon Culture,,
Ocean Bey,,
Los Doses.

*

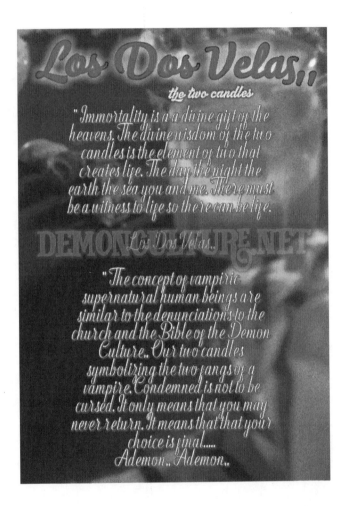

Los Dos Velas,,
the two candles

"Immortality is a a divine gift of the heavens. The divine wisdom of the two candles is the element of two that creates life. The day the night the earth the sea you and me. There must be a witness to life so there can be life.

Los Dos Velas..

"The concept of vampiric supernatural human beings are similar to the denunciations to the church and the Bible of the Demon Culture.. Our two candles symbolizing the two fangs of a vampire.Condemned is not to be cursed. It only means that you may never return. It means that that your choice is final.....
A demon.. A demon..

Let us pray

" *In the name of the Lord the church and the congregation of the demon culture,, May our heavenly joys become our reality. Let not darkness consume us but that we will become one with the unknown dark forces of divinity in the name of Los Dos Velas,, We pray that the judgment shall not fail and eternal life as the deninic angle of our Heavenly Mother shall provide safety, salvation and sanctuary for my soul ad the souls of our famlies,,*

Ademon,, Ademon,,

demonculture.net

The Apocalypse,,

Yahusha,, Yahusha,,

Our Sire,,

"KING DRACULA"

The General,,

Demonculture.net

CHAPTER ELEVEN,,

THE

APOCALYPSE,,

RETRIBUTION

By:

Prime Minister Arnold,,

A Bible of the Demon Culture,,

Los Dos Velas,,

''

Another Chance

Ministries,,

Chapter 1,,

''

The Death Ceremony,,
For the Divine Congregation
of
Los Dos Velas,,

" Bittersweet are the sorrows and the pleasures of life and death. At times life can be cruel even for those who deserve the very best. For this we must count our blessings and protect ourselves with a greater passion. The true gift of life is the gift of after life. The true death only occurs after our death. The wisdom of eternal life and the treasures of immortality are by divinity. The Divine blessings of the Lord's. Our Queen Dracula,, Our Mother Mary,, La virgin de Guadalupe,, La Santa

Muerte,, Our dearest Lord
Mother and Queen. Our
Heavenly Father,, Our Sire,,
Our King Dracula
Our King Jesus,,
However you shall say their
names.
Let us not say them in vain,,

In the Name of Los Dos
Velas,, We Hail to our
Queen, and we Salute to Our
King. We give thanks to The
Divine Supreme,,
As they send forth the
keepers of the souls and the

guardians of the gates to
gather a soul or souls today.
we pray,,

Ademon,, Ademon,,

Let us Pray,,

" In The name of the lord,
the church and the bible of
the
Demon Culture,,
We are gathered here today
in a special celebration. In
the light of the re-birth of
one or more of your special
Children. Today we invite

them home to our divine
spiritual colony of
"Noiisus"
." Here Everyone Lives
Lovely". If you refer to our
home as HELL!! We Hail; to
our Queen
Mother Mary,,

Ademon,, Ademon,,

" As we send forth this
beautiful soul in the light of
truth. By the power invested
in the church the Bible and
the congregation of the
Demon Culture,,

This soul shall live; There is
a front gate to the spiritual
colony of the lord which
leads to the villages and
cities of the Denunic Angels.
My heaven and yours.
Our Heaven of

"Noiisus",,

Chapter 2,,
''

" At this time we will dedicate a plot to pause. In the dark of the grief and the suffering that the family has faced during this dark time and place.

"X6" Ademon,,

" We wish our condolences in the light of new life. With new hope in the hearts of the families that we may heal as their new life begin we honor the commands and shall not sin.,
In the Divine Traditions of Los Dos Velas,,

- "WE COME AGAIN",,

" For he or she who has neither faith nor homage to the lord there are the back gates,,

TAHATUHA,,

The chambers of death and or to Hades. The dark death of religion our ancestors has been purged to due to false instruction. False faith that cursed the Lord and damed us to a spiritual holocaust, but now we are free. Free at last we are free at last. Let freedom, happiness and

bliss for all of eternity be
with this blessed soul as you
have been touched by the
great and divine Rapture of
the Lords,,

Rest Is Peace,,
For the Denunic Angels of
our Lords,,

Ademon,, Ademon,,
And these are our divine
Traditions,,

" Just let us evolve!! Even if. a man was something in the past do not deny him or her the right to change, just because you are scared to do so,,

" You are to refer to me as Mr. Prime Minister Sir,, Or Prime Minister Arnold,,If you are a lady lover of the past, present or future you can call me "Tiger". Do not address me as my birth name. For that is a name not to be spoken. While I was in jail, prison and or homeless on the streets as I am now. I did not receive one letter, visit, call nor penny from not one person, only my mom. So don't say it now or you will be reprehensible for retribution violating the 11th commandment. 1,111 hours of community service for the church will be ordered. Do not use my name in vain,,

" Church Law now reads to never speak the prophet's name in vain. Any talk or display of less than what I have actually done and went through. All that I have lost, suffered and endured. The many years of dark hatred and cold rebuke that fell before me. The many great sacrifices that I have and have yet to take. Say my name in vain For Our King Jesus it's just the same and Ima; Bake You Like A Cake!!,, We

TAHATUHA,,

" Here is what hinders our evolution. My back is hurt. It's hard for me to work. The world demands money that I

don't have so I am homeless.
All them on the streets with
me praise and put all of
their wealth and energy to
drug and alcohol addiction,
so I do this alone. Unable to
watch my own back most of
my creations and equipment
gets stolen. It's sad to say
and it's by the faults of no
other but your own. There
are already missing books of
the bible of the Demon
Culture,, Some cannot be
restored,,

Ademon,, Ademon,,

" Our movement Is of peace
and prosperity. a form of
global Unity that's foreign to
the planet of Earth. My
message is of a Dr Martin
Luther King Jr way of
Direction, to new freedoms
and togetherness as a whole.
Because the blood on the
knife that
kept hitting my back is still
wet I have a Malcolm X way
of doing things, it's not
personal,,

THE
APOCALYPSE,,

" Just because everybody
believes in the same lie does
not make it the truth.
slavery is not always by the
ball in the chain,,

CHAPTER ELEVEN,,

RETRIBUTION,,

By:

Prime Minister Arnold,,

Chapter 3,,
''

" Fear is not written, it is
something that is within
you, it is something that you
control. fear is not within
my character. No the dark is

not fun. A mob full of masked men running at me with guns. I laugh at the thought. Failure for me is the fear in the heart at the time Global Devastation of the innocent children to whom I did not reach with salvation. My reach is not for those of you who live comfortable in America. My reach is for the sick, hungry, poor, and starving children in Africa, Asia, Central and South America, Mexico, Russia, India, China and all other poor countries in the world. I am here for the Salvation of the poor and

the children all around the
globe,,

Denon Culture,,

Los Dos Velas,,

Ademon,, Ademon,,

" It was said to be a dark
Day by the Christian of early
times.

THE
APOCALYPSE,,

" By divine intent this would be the overshadowing of the congregation of the Demon Culture,, Around the entire globe. A dark day, place in time and or event; evil has foreseen of its demise. Mankind has now let the mistreatment of yet another Prophet go way too far. I have kept my head above water for as long as I can. When the heart of our divine Prophet and or spiritual Savior grows cold!! We have the situation that I'm divinely sent here to get us out of. May the lord have mercy for the many good

souls to whom will be left
behind,,

Ademon,, Ademon,,

Los Dos Velas,,

" At times it is better to not
speak than to be looked at
with the eye of rebuke. I am
a clown in spirit now, you
have now made my heart
and soul Dark and cold. A
clown is a warlock, a
powerful Genie!! Now guess

what I am becoming?? Yes
this is the
APOCALYPSE.
I am trying to reach out to
you but you have let me
sink. If I do not speak to you
or I pushed you away from
me it is to protect the planet
and preserve the heavens.
Your hate only makes the
world darker,,

" I only spoke of it before
now but I dehumanize. I am
going to stop letting the
people around me and let
the Bible's teach. I am
becoming a highly evolved

human being of mass
intelligence with no
personality and no spirit. I
feel that I have no success.
Some feel that I have too
much success. I feel that I
am in danger and now I
must protect myself with a
greater passion. I have past,
present and future divine
biblical testament in my
head that We must protect.
For the purity of our future
and our evolution,,

" If you mean us no good,
do not even let me be a
thought of yours. That

thought will plague you and
yours. I will see to all
negative attributes to and
towards my presence. More
so them that do not leave
the mouth but is conceived
by the mind. Them the lord
is witness to as well. Talk
that shit when you get to
H.E.L.L.,,

TAHATUHA,,

" Frank M Perea. who was supposed to be our first apostle at the time. The incarnation of Judas has stabbed the knife far deep within my back. On the criminal complaint that this scripture is written on, He said my name 30 different times to the Albuquerque police department with malicious intent towards me, you and our children. I have lost all that I have but the cloths on my back,,

" I sit with a prevention detention hold on me so I

have no bond. He does this so that he and Jessica M. Shannon, an ex and editor I acquired, could pilfer and prowl through my kindle and amazon accounts. All had to be unpublished. All files stolen of the 9 bibles that were beautifully written for the spiritual safety and salvation of you and your family. Evil people will perish. These two will be placed together in a cell in Hades for all of eternity. The very bottom, to where there is constant pain to the soul in the form of burning. From wall to wall of the glowing red cells deep

within the earth. The halls
look like they never end,,

Demon Culture,,

The
Apocalypse,,

Chapter 4,,
,,

" There is to be no peace on
earth for these two nor to

the families of those who commit crimes against the church!! Neither will there be peace to them who house or employ them. For he or she that does, You will be continuously haunted by the disciples of the lord on earth and in heaven,,

" I depended on my lord to protect me. I am let down to the fact that she didn't or couldn't protect me. So now I depend on my cold heart, my precision and the wrath and fury of the lord's congregation to protect me.

Then I thought about Father
Jesus and his trials and
tribulations. His father did
not protect him either. Now
I understand as I was
ordered by my Queen the
Lords too was ordered by
divinity to not interfere with
the free will of mankind. Let
us dig our own graves even
if it's with the barbaric
treatment of me my death
by murder. This is the final
report for our salvation..

" It is not smart to keep me
in poverty and on the
streets. You're giving your

wealth to them who speak
false religious instruction. If
I must sin to survive I must.
If I lose my soul, I may lose
the souls of you and all of
our children as well. The
heavy heart of a lord can
close the gates to thy
heavens,,

Los Dos Velas,,

Ademon,, Ademon,,

" Is this what the souls of
your children mean to you.

Remember that the heaven
of Christ is closed to the
souls of mankind,,

" The indemnity of my soul
does not rest in your hands.
It is the thousands and
thousands of souls to whom
I have taught, guided and
coached the divine path to
spiritual salvation. Not the
souls on the surface it's the
many souls that dwells in
the dark behind the bushes,
in the allies behind the
dumpsters and even in the
sewers of some
neighborhoods,,

Demon Culture,,

" I am alone in the world. All that I have is the love and support of all of you,, The Congregation of Los Dos Velas,, All sales from the biblical documents goes to the growth and development of the empirical dynasty of the Demon Culture,,

Another Chance Ministries,,

Los Dos Velas,,

" I Just lay in this cell Just as
I did in El Paso Texas with
my face an inch from the
wall all day long. I am in
deep,deep pain in the fear of
losing my good grace with
my lord. To think that my
lord will have such hatred
for me. To think of the fate
of all them to whom I have
led and will lead down the
path to the Lord's spiritual
colony. No!! This cannot be.
If the Queen is Evil; No!! I
will not surrender you to
her. I will be your Saint. I

promise you this. I created
the Religious traditions of
Los Dos Velas,, With the
virtue of global peace,unity
and freedom from evil. If
not by divinity but by ME!!
You will be protected. By
this Bible and the Millions of
people to whom I have
inspired. We will exodus to
whatever spiritual land we
may journey to and we will
have peace, love, happiness
and eternal life, In the name
of the Divine Traditions of

Los Dos Velas,,

" This is my promise to you.
We are not evil and we will
not be evil. The Demon
Culture,, Is not the religion
of the Devil. This is my
religion.

Chanelle Maris Arnold Sr,,

" I created this religion. We
will not be misled by evils. If
the Lord will not protect us.
I will find ways to protect us
by the unity of our great,
proud and beautiful
congregation. Eternal life
shall prevail through the

ways of righteousness. All
Evils weather in the light or
in the dark shall be brought
forth to face the judgment of
the Lord; then shall perish,,

TAHATUHA,,

LOS DOSES,,

" This is the plight of my
existence. This is all l want.
If you think that the design
of my creation and or this

ministry is to avail evil you are wrong. My visionary conquest is not to establish evil. No, I am not trying to build an empire of supernatural demons or evil beings to emperalize and rule the world. Although it does sound cool. That is not the path nor the direction of the Demon Culture,,

Demon Culture,,

" For now I surmise that I am to just endure pain. This pain is now causing me to reshape and to remold my character. I'm ready to submit my final report To the Lord and just let humanity take a bite from the apple of the tree in which it was picked from. You will see the Earth as it was that apple and the destruction you will cause,,

THE
APOCALYPSE,,

Chapter 5,,

''

" It is important for you to
learn the difference between
love and lust. I do not allow

for 1 to tell me that they love
me nor do I use the term.
For one who brings Joy I will
say that I have heart for you.
for amatory and deep
intimate Sensations that
only a woman can bring to
me I will say that I have
passion for her. Love to me
it's betrayal, Twisted Hate
and treachery. Lust is the
attempt to stain my soul
with thin as you have
stained yours into debauche
my salvation. Other than a
child with a grandparent
what great aunt or Uncle
most of them who have told
you that they love you have
cost you a great deal of pain

that it was hard for you to
heal from correctly?
Twisted hate in treachery!
Love is an action not a word.
Do not open your chest and
expose your heart to have a
fistful of dirt tossed into
your open chest. This will
darken the soul which in
turn darkens the rest of
your life,,

'' No I am not gay nor a
homosexual. In fact I hate
and despise them. I have
ordered myself to respond
to them with extremely
merciless distaste.They are

not allowed around me at
all. If you conduct yourself
in this form or manner do
not attempt to approach me
and or enter my Divine
temples. I will place a bet on
you without a thought and
you will be purged from my
presence. Your picture will
be taken and you will see
the master priest,,

Demon Culture,,

" A part of my tribulations I
feel is because either a force
on Earth or within Divinity

wants me to become gay or a faget. This I will never, never do. I will die two times over and the rapture. It is not that important to me to be a fag. f*** NO!! I'll take my chances in the next life. So I say to the Lords and to everybody on Earth. Unless you want to war with me and the entire Congregation of the Demon Culture,, put your fag mask on somebody else. I will never be gay, you cannot force me to be gay, make my mother f****** day,,

" This original scripture is written on a page filed in District Court stating that I have no bond and facing 20 years in prison. I found out yesterday for defending both my manhood and the wealth of our Ministries to a funky ass faget. I will do it again, do not f*** with me ever, ever again,,

" So tell your greedy and faggets friends who attempt to obtain salvation through the Demon Culture,, do not play with their lives like that. I have zero tolerance

for this type of perfidy. You
will be cursed with the
worst type of Retribution it
will be delivered promptly
to the chambers of death ,,

TAHATUHA,,

Chapter 6,,
"

" Calmness is very
important. I cannot tell you
why but during my Odyssey

I just don't happen to be placed into the hands of the nastiest hearted people on this planet. Unfortunately it is these people to whom creates your Bible and are the speakers to Divinity in regards to the Salvation of the world. This is the true life biblical experience of our time. The last of our time. I am very approachable. If you are a good spirited person to come to me and let me know who you are and that you exist. Do not let this come continue to create your Bible and lead us all to death,,

Ademon,, Ademon,,

" No I am not a monster, no I
will not hurt you. Ask
anybody who knows me. I
am a very friendly, creative
and loving person. It is just
the cold hearts and the
treason of them I meet that
makes me close doors to
you. it is the natural instinct
of humans to defend
themselves and all animals
alike. The brutal torture and
murder of the heavenly
father Jesus Christ does

constantly play over and over in my head. I already know my fate. Please do not blame me for defending myself from this; okay,,

" I'm calling it my life insurance policy. I am keeping $1000000 half a million dollars in each grave. I will tell you one last time to keep my name out of your mouth. If for whatever reason my name is given to any law enforcement agency and or placed on any note and or criminal complaint of any kind I want the tongue

of that person and their
closest kin in a bag in
exchange for the name on
the grave or Graves,,

" I'm in the hole right now
solitary confinement seg-5
at M.D.C. I am not here for
discipline. I am here by
personal request. 23-hour
lockdown. I don't want the
other one out so 24-hour
lockdown. I do not want any
human contact at all, at all. I
now grow dark and cold. It
seems the illogical but
however since the beginning

this has been the only
defense for evil,,

" You did this to yourself by
standing back, being a
coward and letting slimy
people direct the path of
your spiritual salvation. I
cannot promise you that
everything is going to be
okay. I do not know when it
is all said and done if you
will live. Where is your
heart towards the Lord and
towards the
Commandments of the
Lord? Think about this one,
you will hear this again at

the time of your ultimate
judgment,,

Los Dos Velas,,

" You know that I turned
Itchy. Itchy Clown Buksmg,,
Itchy to the 111th
Degree,,What it means to be
itchy is to want it now and
to sacrifice it all to get it.
Just like when you itch some
place on your body. The
irritation of that itch has
you seek to cure and or
alleviate that discomfort
immediately. I want my

spiritual and financial
Independence now. I want
my motherfuking money
now and I'm itchy for it to
the hundred 111th Degree,,
it is wise for you not to get
in my way. However it is
healthy for your soul to
contribute,,

" I have created a praetorian
prototype by the name of
Aming. This prototype is
now in Juarez Chihuahua
Mexico for refinements.
These waist hide Android
militant robots will serve as
C.P.O. 's . Church peace

officers in light of to Serve
and Protect the
congregation of the Lord
Los Dos Velas,,

" This is chapter 11,, I
remind you that all chapter
11 Bibles of the demon
culture or of a personal
Conquest. They are
synonymous with all of the
Testament in light of global
retribution. This is of my
own volition. I can feel the
tears of the Lord falling
upon my soul when I am
riding some of these
scriptures of chapter 11,,

THE
APOCALYPSE,,

" We only spoke of the
creation of the praetorium
prototypes in chapter 11 the
hundred and 11th degree.
Now you have witnessed the
creation of the first. This is

why the 11th chapter of all
chapter 11 bibles are blank.
You get to watch happen the
ultimate chapter of live. I'm
not playing I intend to do or
have done every single last
page of the Bible's of the
Demon Culture,, This is the
true life biblical experience
of our time,,
Demon Culture,,

LOS DOSES,,

" I have written out the
Declaration of church and

state of the Demon Culture,,
I have a photo of me holding
a wooden sign with the AC
painted in blue. I have
written this Divine
document announcing our
Liberation. This is the
amendment of our ultimate
liberation. In manila
envelopes ready to send to
world leaders all over the
globe. An Urgent friendly
informal inclosed on the
front of each envelope
highlighted in red,,

Chapter 7,,
‘’

" I do not want any human
contact as of now. Your love
for me it's fake and your
treason upon me is
imminent. I will not

continue the Rapture until I
have my home. I have no
wealth so I am going to the
heart of Juarez Chihuahua
Mexico. With nothing but
my faith I am going to this
Wasteland with my chest of
Bibles in search of a home
and a place to find me build
my church,,

" Even if it is falling apart,
full of green and black mold,
and it is full of alligators,
snakes or bands of renegade
killers in them. I am picking

one to be my home. The
ministry's is dead until then
I have not one word or heart
nor passion for not one of
you until I am secure you
have a home and I am
married and can celebrate
the Divine traditions of Los
Dos Velas,, in matrimonial
Harmony,,

" Now when I have my home
I will be like brother
Malcolm X in the window
with this AK-47 but they
Itchy clown mask on when
Darkness Falls,,

'' They will act like they are
members of the church to
me. They will feel like they
are members of the church.
This is always the beginning
of a major downfall for me. I
am alone in the world and
it's easy to Target me for
drug, gang and criminal
activity. It is all fake love
with the means to destroy
surreptitiously. But to some
this is their way of showing
affection to numb the pain
of being lost. Ignorant to
who they truly are,,

" It is sad now that my scripture is now based on your greed, evil and hatred towards me instead of my love for my Lord and your spiritual salvation. Salvation that will open the gates to the land of immortality to and for The Souls of mankind to live for eternity,,

" It is sad that I must live alone in the darkness because you as mankind feel that the already hard-earned dollar of a profit must be spent on your

junky ass addictions. The
Lord sends me to you the
children and the port to
coach and guide to the
Divine path to spiritual
salvation and you act like
you are listening but lurking
to take my last dollar for
your drugs and drinking,,

" There is no devil, only the
monster that you create
within yourself. The Lord's
are Our Mother Mary and
Father Jesus. When you
worship one the other will
then challenge your faith.
For I am a jealous Lord

written biblically for both
the mother and the father.
This explains the challenges
you face in life and the
relation to your praise and
worship. Do not give up or
give in to the deception of
the other Lord,,

" Over half of the citizens of
the planet of Earth have a
place in the spiritual colony
of the Lord and they're place
in the rapture of the Lord.
The majority of the world is
in poverty, and or are
innocent children. It is your
souls to whom I am sent

here to rapture. I do feel as
if I am obligated to coach
you all in this direction.
However I do not feel
obligated to endure hatred,
rebuke and to be falsely
persecuted for my godly
efforts for you,,

" What has come in the past
will come again in the
future. Just as the Earth is
round what goes around will
come back around. This is
the structure of evolution
for most Prophets; this is
how we can tell what will
happen in the future. I

already got my memorial
tattooed on my back fully
equipped with The walking
Dead Kamikaze mutherfuka
and the clown on the cross
already for you,,

" It was said that the Lord
took over half of a
congregation of already
angels in heaven into the
darkness with her. My task
is no less than what has
been done before. I am here
to serve in her honor. She is
here to do the exact same
thing here on Earth as was
done before in the heavens,,

Demon Culture,,

Los Dos Velas,,

Ademon,, Ademon,,

" The evil and the hate of the
Christian of early times is
just as strong as it was
yesterday. They just use
different weapons to
slaughter the cultural races
of people. Now that use
liquor, drugs, sex and the

number one weapon of
mass destruction of the
human spirit is their sword;
the holy Bible,,

Chapter 8,,
''

" Then they will see no
more. Most of the of the
Lord's Denunic angles are
the souls of children. Our
Heavenly Mother and her

beautiful children are the
family of mine's. There are
adult Angels as well but very
few, will you be one of
them,,

Los Dos Velas,,

" I just denunced Navajo
brother Patrick Shay the
dine way, Los Doses,, in the
pod E-8 M.D.C. A powerful
spirited man. One of the
very few cell mates I have
had who didn't flinch nor
move cells when I began to
share the wisdom of the

Lord. A seat among the hierarchy of the Ministries will be held in his honor,,

" I am trying to leave now to continue the rapture. The seed of the ministry is planet very well in the belly of the beast the middle of the United States,,

" I will travel next to Juarez Chihuahua Mexico. Here in the US will only keep me here. Until that soul is completely free with the

wisdom I share. The
questions and the search for
knowledge and wisdom will
send silent prayers to the
Lord. She will then send me
or keep me to silence these
prayers and guide
successfully these souls
To her colony,,

" You cannot miss treat me
and no I cannot miss treat
you. Treason upon my heart
is treason upon the heart of
the Lord. To dehumanize
and two grow dark and cold
is just the shock of that
initial threat and or the

perfidious crimes against the church. I haven't even begun to unveil the true power that is invested in me. I am sure that I also have powers and or special gift that I am not aware of. At the full might of my Force, may the Lord forbid!! I can possibly drag the entire planet of Earth into a deep, dark depression that will touch the hearts and souls of every last person on the planet,,

Ademon,, Ademon,,

The
APOCALYPSE,,

" It is the most epic thing to do for the human spirit. The denunciations to the church the Bible and the Congregation of Los Dos Velas,,

" Crimes against the church
shall not go unpunished. It
is now up to the
congregation to bring
justice and attempt to
restore the good virtue of
our Prophet and spiritual
Savior. We are a pure
religion without the sin of
war holding us back from
salvation. We are still a
religion free of war, We will
always be. For this reason I
an relentless In My efforts,,

" I will fight all of our battles
single handedly, With the

wrath of the heavens behind
me. No opposition means no
war. No war equals? ?
World Peace,,

Demon Culture,,

Chapter 9,.
''

Los Doses,,

" Do you know what a
Zombie Apocalypse looks
like??

" Now imagine this on a
global scale. All over the
world. Food for thought the
religion of Los Dos Velas is
now a world religion!! There
are now members of the
Demon Culture,, All around
the world!! This is just a
small mental preview of
chapter 10 of this divine

biblical document. Going to 111 from 2 in just a few seconds, just to keep your interest at peak. Now i'm going to talk a little shit,,

THE

APOCALYPSE,,

" There are going to be a few things that I'm going to need. This is not a hostage situation by far,,

This is Chapter Eleven,,

" Bankruptcy for the rich,evil and greedy Christians!! You are getting richer by teaching false religion and daming us to face the Lord with bitterness in her hearts for us. Fuck Me!! No Fuck You!! Your giving all that money back to the people and making a confession. I'm not here to negotiate, I'm here to liberate!! Time to pay the pauper. The meek shall inherit the earth,,

Demon Culture,,

Los Dos Velas,,

Ademon,, Ademon,,

" I need the means to reach
the hearts and the souls of
the sick, hungry, poor and
starving children around the
world. I do not want no gold,
big houses, fancy cars or
none of that shit. I need the
divine teachings of the lord,
"The Bibles of the Demon
Culture" Mandatory to every

ear on the planet of earth.
Then let us decide
altogether what is true and
divine. (Heavenly),,

LOS DOSES,,

" So rebuke me if you will.
That's ok with me. What
man rebukes has no
relevance to religion nor
principle to divinity. Man
rebuked Jesus Christ in his
time as well. You can take all
that rebuke and pile it all up
in a big ball and hold it in
your arms. Now you can go
stand at the end of the long

ass line of them who hate
and rebuke me, Perfect. Now
we turn this line into the
first line of muthafuckas i'm
going to be throwing in the
ovens
Extra Crispy,,

TAHATUHA,,

" Not only do I hold the keys
to the lord's spiritual colony.
I hold the keys to the
chambers of death as well. I
have Zero tolerance for a
nuisance. This is not a game

and I'm not here to play with you. If you want to play, go and play with your kids at home. Do not attempt to play with me. They are soon to be playing and listening to Itchy Clown Buksmg toys, and Itchy's Gun house!! Ha, Ha, Ha, ME,,

" It is the example the United States government wants to leave upon the entire world. All Prophets, spiritual leaders and all other liberators of mankind alike have been accused of crimes and persecuted by this government. It was the descendants of this same government that tried and executed our Heavenly Father. The direct meaning of this is to show the world that not even (GOD) is above The United States Government,,

" This is what makes me seem so dark and cold. I do group punishment. I have no help. I am alone in this massive liberation of mankind. I have hatred and rebuke constantly raining

down upon me. I have no
room for a mistake. This
divine spiritual movement is
the reshaping of the
heavens. One wrong shift
turns our promise land into
what?? Understand,,

Los Dos Velas,,

Ademon,, Ademon,,

" You rebuke me for being
dark and cold, well I have
poverty and very little family
support. I am broke and
alone. You may have money
and a family. A family is all I

truly want.I will not accept being a part of a family not of Los Dos Velas,, I stay and pray where I know I am safe,,

Demon Culture,,

" A promise to you and not a threat. To anybody who takes even a penny of the church's money!! I have spent every penny I have ever gotten on you and your family's salvation. Do not play with your soul like this.

Go and steal from the
Christians!! They got all the
money. They are stealing
from you; not me,,

Chapter 10,,
",

" To the Congregation of
the lord. At times we have a
hard time getting the ear of
someone important to us.
Write them a letter. They
will talk to you without a
shield,,

Los Dos Velas,,

'' The Bible's of the Demon Culture,, Are love letters to Our Beloved Lord Mother and Queen. They are to beseech her for the Divine Gift of Immortality for the entire congregation of,,

Los Dos Velas,,

The

Demon Culture,,

Another Chance Ministries,,

LOS DOSES,

" Los Dos Velas,,

Demon Culture,,

"

Chapter 11,,

"'

Chapter Eleven

Chapter Eleven

The Apocalypse,,

Chapter Eleven

The Apocalypse,,

Chapter Eleven

The Apocalypse,,

Chapter Eleven

The Apocalypse,,

Chapter Eleven

The Apocalypse,,

Chapter Eleven

The Apocalypse,,

Chapter Eleven

The Apocalypse,,

Chapter Eleven

The Apocalypse,,

Chapter Eleven

The Apocalypse,,

Chapter Eleven

The Apocalypse,,

Chapter Eleven

The Apocalypse,,

Chapter Eleven

In the Name of
Los Dos Velas,,

": No I will not surrender
you to evil. I will be your
Saint. I Promise you this. I
created the Religion of the
Demon Culture,, With the
virtue of global peace, unity
and freedom from evil. If
not by divinity but by ME!!
You will be protected by this
bible and the millions of
people to whom I have
inspired. We will exodus to

whatever spiritual land we
may journey to and we will
have peace, love, happiness
and eternal life, In the name
of the divine traditions of,,

Los Dos Velas,,

Ademon,, Ademon,,

'' This is my promice as
your Divine prophet and
spiritual savior,,

Prime Minister Arnold,,

The Apocalypse,,

Made in the USA
Columbia, SC
11 February 2024

31258103R00076